I0418343

# The Mean Reds

# *The Mean Reds*

Jillian M. Phillips

Copyright 2025: Villainess Press

ISBN: 979-8-9919596-1-2

Book Design & Cover Art: Copyright 2025 Jillian M. Phillips

All rights reserved. No part of this book may be used or reproduced in any manner for the purpose of training artificial intelligence technologies or systems.

# TABLE OF CONTENTS

Listen to the Playlist/Soundtrack for *The Mean Reds* on Spotify!!

Scan QR Code
or visit:

*https://tinyurl.com/ywj8nwex*

*DEDICATION*

*To my girls, my mother, and "those women."*

"The blues are because you're getting fat, and maybe it's been raining too long. You're just sad, that's all. The mean reds are horrible. Suddenly you're afraid, and you don't know what you're afraid of."

— Truman Capote, *Breakfast at Tiffany's*

# The L Words

## *Work on Command*

You try and you laugh.
You beauty and you adjective.
And then, there is more hiding

because you have painted a picture
of flowers while trying to swallow
nightshade and foxglove,

made poems like balloon animals,
felt the prick of the pin
and tried to press harder, to pop.

You make and you breathe.
You create and you birth.
And then, the calendar moans

because it is not enough to verb
and noun your heart into obscurity,
you must blood and tear.

## To a First Love

Ours is a way-done love
a long-time-gone love
A saw-it-in-the-street-and-kicked-it-like-a-soda-can love

When we were kids, we caught tadpoles
and stored them in ice cream buckets
in your mother's garage.
We had a setting-pollywogs-free-in-the-pond type love,
hoped they'd become frogs we could keep as pets later.

It was a Skid-Row/Poison-mix-tape love,
a playing-Nintendo-then-House-then-I-hate-you kind of
love.

It's a way-done, wonder-what-happened-to-you love,
an I-showed-you-mine-you-showed-me-yours love,
a we'll-keep-it-cool-at-recess love.

I heard you were arrested about ten years ago,
drugs or fighting, and I thought about your mother
and how she used to laugh with my mother,
and how they had a single-mother-neighbor-kindred kind
of love.

4

Ours is way done, an I'll-remember-you-with-fondness
love,

a we-were-just-kids love,

an I-still-catch-tadpoles-with-my-kids love.

## *I Did Not Know How to Cry Back Then*

I was full of *fuckyous* and *lovemes*.
I yanked the stars out of your eyes

so you could see me clearly;
an untainted view of my landscape.

Gently, I would tease your neck with my tongue
and fight the urge to sink my teeth in.

## We Could Burn Ourselves Down with Knowing

Faces peer through windows,
afflicted with silence,

half blind, half hungry.
Craving thought,

I suck on meaning like it's candy.
I watch words, like ghosts,

pierce the air with invisible fists.
See them, know intention.

### *I conjure you in images*

Molecularly,
You are water
and acid.

Visceral and immediate,
I see you in soap bars
and wrenches.

The exact moment I loved you:
Roast beef sandwiches,
Passenger seat,
Abbe Hill Drive.

Olfactorily,
You are grease
and sweat.

I threw a box across the room:
Toy
Aircraft carrier
Pills

Slash sounds
like an open wound:

Auditorily,
You are sweet moans
and dissonance.

## *Antistrophe*

Your voice has always been the trigger
as I've stood against your firing squad.
There is effort in remaining still,
strain in staying silent.

You, your sentence,
the original strophe chorus.
A man, you have been many men
gathering with your hot bullets,
hands all over my gun belt.

If I were a playwright,
I could not neglect the women
moving in the opposite direction.

Every time you have been still,
I have studied you.
Every time you have been silent,
I have listened to your breathing.

Some plays end with
both sides dying
because neither side could win.

## I Remember Things That May Not Be True

I remember that you
were a fish
gasping for water
when all I had to give was air
I remember that I was a teacher
in Nazi Germany

I remember a foot massage in a bar
sex by the roaring dam
and Indian food in China
before I remember that
neither of us likes curry
and we have no passports.

But, you were a builder of bombs
and slept in the desert.
But was I the napkin you used
to wipe your mouth
or was I the tongue
that made your mouth dirty?

I recall you made chocolate chip cookies
and lent me a vacuum cleaner
when I was a beekeeper
and you were a tailor

I was stung by your arms.
I think you were a lumberjack.
I remember you tasting
like metal
and wood.
I was a virgin,
or a Virgo. .

If we took a test
We got A's, got drunk
on our own genius.
The dog slept on the pile of clothes
next to your bed.
I lost my underwear at some point;
found it in the kennel.

I was mauled by a window dressing.
You were a cup of coffee
and a Band-Aid

I remember our time as circus freaks,
as horses.
A mechanic and a waitress

rowing a defunct canoe
through a busy Walmart.

It was December,
almost Christmas,
and I was corpse
or an embryo

## Looking Better on the Floor

The creases tell the wear
of the shirt, where the elbows
were bent to cross the arms
across a heaving chest.

The collar is tinged brown,
that's where the sweat was,
where the perfume rubbed away
leaving faint whispers
of freesias and lilies,
an archeological dig for scent.

Gaping buttonholes show
that no one cared to be careful,
wanted the shirt off
without messing up their hair.

The cuffs are still rolled
as if someone pushed them up
to cool off in the midday sun
or ready themselves for a fight.

## Like A Head

He'll rub you smooth,
worry you like a stone
down to a worn-out gleam.

And while he calls you Precious Jewel
he'll pump and thrust you purple,
make his own amethyst trophy.
He'll mount you, stuff you

until you're so full of him
your organs are cotton

and your eyes stare blankly
at the opposite wall.

You'll call this love,
engrave your own nameplate
for his prize mausoleum.

### *Your Side of the Bed, Silent*

Sheets, not tumbled,
don't dance anymore,
not the way they used to.
Not the way they laughed
with movement.

So straight, so white,
so quiet, so angry
with stillness.

## What Was Left

He could have slammed the cupboard doors,
thrown chairs, broken glasses,
left her to pick up the shards with bloody hands.

He could have left a wake of torn clothes,
unmade bed, dented walls,
left her to patch the holes herself.

He could have slapped her occasionally,
left her cheek mountainous and purple,
so the swelling could explain his absence.

Invisible pain always bleeds more;
the scars they can't see
take the longest to heal.

## Do I Have to Wish You Joy?

When a man is saved from drowning,
does he pray for the lake to find peace?

I would look at the water, imagine
floating bloating and blue. Think, *Almost.*

## Extract

I have not memorized you,

cannot get your vowels
to settle themselves
in neat little rows
on my tongue,
all-black shininess,
ammunition poised
to rhyme inside the holes
it creates.

Constant consonants
roll around in my cheeks
like ball bearings,
silver balls bearing
the weight of you
caught in the back
of my throat.

It might be easier
to swallow this
garble of poetry
than trip over my teeth
and wallow, worrying

that it's not that
I haven't memorized you
but have begun to forget

the way you taste.

## *I Will Write You*

At some point, I will

write you as the poem

I need you to be.

I need you to be

forgiveness, the ghost

of a word. The ghost

I made of myself,

letting you (the concrete)

haunt me (the abstract).

I will abstract you

into extraction,

my precise excision.

I will make you

to the point of unmaking.

The point of unmaking is

(of course) exorcism,

an exercise in ridding.

So you will not be the pot,

the broken flower pot,

or the astronaut

to my moon landing.

I am not the moon,

never was cosmic

or (even slightly) the atmosphere.

I fear

your breath. Your breath
was always labor,
because you labored me
to love you.
I am not birth,
you are not womb.
Someday,
you will be a poem.

## *You've Become A Reverie*

She tends to dream in cliché
when the dream is about you.

Your poetry doesn't
make her uncomfortable.

She craves punishment for moving beyond you.
She always felt

she was a better poet than you.
She'd never tell you you're her favorite ghost.

She dreams there are woods
and the strip mall is a cabin

and the mo(u)rning birds are singing.
She feels she deserves it.

And that's half the reason
she still dreams about you:

being haunted reminds her
she isn't a good person.

## Cemetery

My dreams are graveyards
haunted by loves lost,
fears realized.

I have erected monuments
to my mistakes, mossed over
and filmed with haze.

Shrouded and shrill,
the dead memories dance,
cobwebs on their fingers,

tickling the peace away,
reminding me I never mourned
moving on, only
buried the roads.

## Ghost Language

And if it is our dead bringing silence, so what?
What more crying in their absence does it matter?

As if they'll hear us better when
we scream into the shadows they left behind?

And if our dead are the echoes,
what is the sound we are making
for their ghosts to hang onto?

No more living are we doing than the ghosts
if we are still talking to the dead.

If it is ours to mourn, why do we choose
to stop moving, to sit beside their graves
and make confessions?

And if our dead knew what we didn't say,
would they still be living?
Would an apology equal a month of life?
A profession of love, a decade?
What does our presence *now*
mean for the dead *then*?

It's not resurrection for them we are seeking,

but second chances for ourselves,

because we fear missing out

on absolution.

*Mother, Mother*

## Igneous Child

(Ash-covered or magma'ed)
Once he was your lava:
all gold tongue
wet, leather zipper's friction.
His fruition was fat,
loved you to a stretch mark
graveyard. He's the ghost
haunting you
every time you look at me.
I'm your Pompeii:
beautiful island, melted,
relic of itself.
I've always known
I was a natural disaster.
Hot liquid, hardened,
I cooled everything.

## *Confession*

I should have been a quiet girl,
could have been obedient
by being invisible;
when you made me disappear,
my absence wouldn't have been
so loud. I never listened.

## On Her Precipice

My daughter is twelve,
waiting for her period

to punctuate the sentence
of her childhood,

anxious to end the imperative
and start asking questions.

Growing up is a commencement,
not graduating,           .
                    *beginning.*

## The Upheaval

You've become seismic.
I feel you quaking,

creating fissures in the world.
It breaks me apart, too.

This chasm you leave:
I know it's meant for me.

## Confession #2

I could have loved you more.
  Should have,
    in fact. But I,

I was a tea leaf steeping
  in my own hate.
    Poor cookie,

    you went stale
before I could save you
  for later.

## Blood Desert

I tied you to a red string.
You have always been trailed by red.

A woman is made redder until
she is maroon-black, and all is dry.
Do not become the blood desert.

I tied you tightly once, unflown kite,
crimson morning, sailing nightmare.
You swallow too much wind. Blow away.

Where it's cold, the numbing ignores
the knots, the acrid anger.
You will be darker and used.

Hold tight. Hang onto me.
I unravel but my threads
are strong. I won't let go.

## Confession #3

They say babies can hear in the womb.
When you were cradling nubs, gelatinous webbing,
knotting an organ blanket,
you heard me wrong;

I was fighting for you.
My body rejected you least of all:
your cord around my neck, love noose,
placental bell jar. Blood just bleeds;
only people under the glass shatter.

# How To Get Through It

*Step One*

Realize two days after Christmas that your period is late. Triple check the calendar, just to be sure. Call the only friend you know that isn't working today and ask her to drive you to the Planned Parenthood on Main Street.

When you get there, keep your head down, hoping that no one you know sees you. You don't want to explain that you are neurotic about your flow and are too poor to buy an eight-dollar pregnancy test. Thank God Planned Parenthood is free.

When the doctor comes in and confirms that you are pregnant, hide your smile. Try to appear appropriately distressed because you are not married, and don't want her to think you are a slut or a welfare queen. Nod along to everything she says. Pretend that you are interested in "Options." Accept every pamphlet gratefully and solemnly, as if each one contains a sacred promise.

When your friend drives you home, share the news with her. Allow her to see your joy, but don't tell anyone else. You know how hard your life has been lately. Your rent is way overdue. You've received two disconnection notices from the power company. You don't want people telling you that your baby is a mistake. You don't want it to be a problem people tell you to fix. Rationalize that you have eight more months to be in a better apartment in a better neighborhood. Your boyfriend, M, has a new job. If you watch your budget carefully, you can save enough to get a nicer place.

*Step Two*

Write in your journal about how excited you are. You know this baby will be a boy. Name him Caleb. Picture him with black hair, shiny as steel, and gray-blue eyes that glow like a stormy sky.

See him in your mind as a voracious reader with a contemplative nature. He will be a poet. He will have a strong will. He will speak softly, but firmly, and use literary quotes in everyday conversation.

Decide that you are unwilling to allow M any say in this pregnancy, because he will tell you to get rid of it. He'll tell you that you are financially unstable, barely able to take care of yourself, not ready.

Write in your journal that you will wait until your second trimester, when you can't legally terminate the pregnancy. It's only two months away. You can keep your mouth shut for that long.

*Step Three*

Call yourself an idiot for leaving your journal open on the kitchen table while you were cooking dinner. Curse your stupidity at not putting it away in your nightstand, where it belonged, instead of letting M find it.

Now he knows you're pregnant. He tells you exactly what you thought he would and is even angrier because he knows you were planning to lie to him.

M tells you to "do what's right." He reminds you that you have always been Pro-Choice. Curse yourself again for not having strong enough faith in your religion to hide behind. You have no argument other than you've already come up with a name. The moment you rolled the syllables around in your mouth and felt them on your tongue, pregnancy ceased to be an abstract concept. Caleb is no longer a scientific term—embryo, zygote. He's a *person* to you.

Listen to M's argument. Let him pace around the living room as he rants on and on that you can barely put food in

41

your own mouths, let alone a child's. In a self-satisfied, fuck-you tone of voice, tell him that you are planning to breastfeed, which negates his argument. Casually add that *he* was the one who didn't put on a condom. This is his fault as much as yours. He ignores this, of course, and turns it back on you. *You* always forget to take your birth control pill on time. One simple thing and you can't even do that, he says. Mutter something about subconscious intentions.

When he says that there is no extra money coming in to save up for the new apartment you're planning on, remind him that you are up for a supervisor position at work. If they pass you over for the position, because you will need maternity leave, you will have even more money from the settlement you'll get by suing them for discrimination under the Family Medical Leave Act. You don't know that this is actually a viable option, but you are already running out of defenses. After all, the only argument you planned on was when M found out too late. When that happened, you were going to say you didn't notice, or had found spotting in your underwear and assumed you just were having a light month.

You're good at playing stupid. Even better at lying. It would have worked.

Finally, tell M that he can choose to be a father or choose to be a deadbeat dad. You can be a parent by yourself. You don't need him. This isn't entirely true. You don't know if you can live on your own, because you never have. You've always depended on someone to help you. But you figure your mother raised you by herself, and even though you grew up on welfare, your mother always made sure you had dance lessons and decent clothes. Promise yourself that you can do that too.

Say it again: you don't need him. Try to mean it. Try to convince yourself of your independence and strength as much as you're trying to convince M. When he calls you stupid, call him a pessimist. It's the strongest word you can think of.


*Step Four*

After resolving to ignore M's constant berating, put up with three days of him telling you you're wrong. Remind him that it's *your* decision, not his. It's *your* body, not his. Wish that you could also tell him the baby wasn't his, so he'd stop arguing. There's no use. You've never cheated on him and he knows it. You wouldn't know who to sleep with even if you wanted to cheat.

*Step Five*

On New Year's Eve, have another argument, following the same script, but this time, *cry*.

Cry because you are frustrated. You can't believe that M refuses to see your side. He refuses to imagine holding his son for the first time, admiring his café-au-lait skin and content, almond-shaped
eyes. He refuses to think about the wondrous moment when Caleb will wrap his pudgy hand around his pinky finger, making him beam with pride. After two hours, he walks away, drowns you out with the radio in the bedroom.

You're hungry. Caleb is already beginning to affect your appetite. Go to the kitchen. When you turn on the light, catch a brown flutter of movement in the corner of your eye.

Turn the light off.

Sharply inhale and feel your heartbeat quicken. Feel it pound
inside your chest so hard that you're sure it's beating against
your ribs. It punches so hard, you're sure it's trying to escape
your body.

Stand still.

Count to ten, as slowly as you can.

*One, one thousand. Two, one thousand.*

Feel the numbers whistle through your teeth as you whisper
them.

Turn the light back on.

This time, you have an extra moment to see what it is, in the corner, because you know where to look. The brown mass is shiny, moving in a swift, smooth way. Its disappearance is quick, but you've seen enough.

*Cockroaches.* There could've been anywhere from twenty to a hundred. You don't care. One would have been enough. The clicking of their hard bodies rubbing against each other as they tried to escape the light rings in your ears. Each *tlik-tlik* blends with another, forming a sick slithering sound. For a split second, think of the ocean. How each droplet of water joins with another to create a cacophonous *whoosh* with the tide.

Stare at the crack in the wall they escaped into. As the bile of disgust rises in your throat, grab the closest thing to you and hurl it across the kitchen. When it lands, look at what you threw. It was your journal, still open to the same page M read. You're too exhausted to smirk at the irony.

Turn off the light. You're not hungry anymore. Go into the living room and lay down on the couch.

As people begin to cheer in the apartment above you, realize it's midnight. It's the New Year. Wish you had a television so you could see the party in Times Square and admire Dick Clark's ability to look the same as he did on the American Bandstand reruns you used to watch after school.

Start to think of all the things you don't have. No television. No dependable heat; your radiator wasn't working so the landlord gave you three space heaters to keep warm. Your electric bill was more than your rent last month.

The next one will be even higher with the snowstorm coming next week. You have no money to pay the electric company. You have no way to do laundry because you can never save enough quarters to go to the Laundromat. You washed your work clothes in the shower last week because you don't even have a bathtub.

Lay on that couch, in the dark, and keep thinking about how awful your apartment is. You had convinced yourself that it was temporary, not so bad for an in-between place. Think to yourself that, maybe, M is right. If you have this baby— you can't call him Caleb as you think this—you'll never leave this place. You'll be forcing yourself into permanent poverty.

Any baby you raise here will never forgive you for being poor. He won't forgive you when the crack in the window finally gives way and lets the bitter wind rush in. He won't forgive you when a cockroach scuttles across his face one night. He will always wonder how you could allow yourself to remain in such pathetic squalor that you once found a crack pipe when you tried to fix a tile in the drop-ceiling. You once listened to a neighbor sell her friend painkillers just outside your door.

Within five minutes of finding your kitchen infested with vermin, change your mind from fervently in favor of keeping your baby to resigned acceptance of what you know you need to do. Start crying again. Let your body rack with sobs as you apologize over and over to Caleb. Shake so violently that you break into a sweat. When you cry so hard that mucus runs from your nose into your mouth and chokes you, do not notice it.

Close your eyes because they're sore and beginning to swell against your tears.

Become numb to every sensory stimulation: the *thwop-plink* of the drippy faucet, the scratch of the wool blanket covering you, M's snoring.

Exist for an hour in the thunderous rush of silence that your decision has brought. Hear nothing but your own guilt. Taste nothing but hiccups as you struggle to breathe normally. Feel nothing but the twist in your stomach, as it tries to wring the blame out of itself, as if it were a wet washcloth.

You are more alone in this moment than you have ever been.

Feel the tears coming back immediately, the lump rising in your throat. Go to the bathroom. Run the water as cold as you can. Put the stopper in the drain so the bowl fills.

Submerge your face in the iciness. Someone once told you that it always helps when you need to calm down. The cold shocks you. The skin on your face tightens immediately. Feel tempted to drown yourself in the freezing water. Realize that you wouldn't be able to stand over the sink long enough for it to work.

*Step Six*

On January 2$^{nd}$, dig into the bottom of your purse for the pamphlets the doctor gave you at Planned Parenthood. Find the number for Danbury Women's Clinic. It's one of only two clinics in the state that perform The Procedure. The lady who picks up the phone sounds bored. She probably thinks you're another girl from the projects whose baby daddy's identity is up for debate. (Years later, you'll be ashamed of the stereotypes you currently hold. About thinking that of other people, perpetuating the prejudice, and calling yourself the same names.)

Resist the urge to blurt out that this is your first and only time, and that you're really a good person who isn't totally sure she should be doing this.

She sets an appointment for you. You're grateful that it's soon.

*Step Seven*

Wake up at five-thirty in the morning on January 13th. It's a Saturday, so the traffic won't be too bad; it should only take an hour and a half to get there. Your appointment is eight.

M drives. He passes the clinic three times before you finally see it. It's a small, square, stucco building with a little parking lot behind it. There's no sign on the building. Reason that they probably made it hard to find on purpose:

one, to discourage women from finding and using it and, two, to make it hard for the protestors to identify as a target.

Sign in. The receptionist tells you that you will meet with a counselor first. Find this unnecessary but agree because it's part of The Process. They have to make sure that you're doing this for the "Right Reasons." That you're not using them for birth control. Really, you just made a mistake.

Wait almost half an hour to be called back by the counselor. She has a generic, upbeat name—Sandy, Cindy, Katie, something like that—and a kind smile. Her eyes and voice are equally concerned. She asks if you are being forced to make this decision. You want to tell her yes. You don't want this. You hate being here. You'll figure it out somehow.

Lose your nerve. Remember how cold it was last night with the bitter wind whistling in through the cracked window and under the front door. It was only fifty degrees in your apartment.

While she rambles on about Life Choices and Methods of Support, fix your eyes on a basket of colorful stones on the table next to your chair. Pick up a bright purple one. It's the perfect shade, not too pink, not flirting with being magenta. Roll it between your thumb and forefinger. The counselor tells you that you can keep it. Look up at her, confused.

"The stone," she says. "You can keep it." She explains that some girls like to have something to do with their hands while they wait.

After another twenty minutes of discussing your situation and decision, the counselor says it's okay for you have The Procedure. Feel like you passed a psychiatric evaluation.

Realize that's *exactly* what you did.

You are sane. You are rational. *Deserving.* This doesn't make you feel any better, but it's good to know.

*Step Eight*

Wait another hour in the main lobby. The walls are covered in cheap-looking, shiny wallpaper. Cream and rose stripes alternate across all four walls. Someone has stenciled moss-green ivy leaves around the reception window so the woman at the desk looks like she's sitting in a picture frame.

Try to read some magazines. You brought a book of 19th Century poetry so people seeing you read it would think you were a smart girl, maybe even a Yale-y, not some hopeless case living in the slums. You tried reading it, but you couldn't concentrate on the complex rhythms. You picked up the magazine closest to you. You can barely focus on *Good Housekeeping's* "24 Ways to Maximize Your Space".

Stare at the girl sitting directly across from you. She's about your age. She's reading *Seventeen* and chatting happily with her boyfriend. You can't believe she's acting as if nothing is wrong. How is she not crying? How is she able to remain completely oblivious to the atmosphere in the room? How is she the only one who isn't solemn and scared? You've been on the verge of tears all morning; not only are her eyes dry and white, but she's managed to apply a full face of makeup this morning. Find this unfair. Hope she's just here to refill her birth control or get a pap smear.

You were the second person to arrive this morning, but the waiting room is steadily filling with more girls. Most are with their mothers; some barely look old enough to be in high school. You and the happy girl are the only two with men. One of the younger girls has a wild look in her eyes. Her mother's lips are pressed together so tightly that only a thin white line suggests her mouth. She's reading a pamphlet. Wonder if it's the same one the counselor gave you about how to take care of yourself afterwards.

A head pokes out from behind a door next to the reception area. It's a nurse. She calls your name. Look at M. Plead with your eyes, *Don't let me do this. Change your mind.*

He squeezes your hand.

Stand up.

Walk slowly.

*Step Nine*

Follow the nurse through the door down a short hallway. Reach into your pocket and close your fingers around the purple stone. Press your thumb into its small grooves.

Breathe. Pass a lounge filled with large, plush armchairs and two televisions tuned to MTV.

"That's the recovery area," the nurse tells you.

Nod once, slowly, to signal you understand. Walk into the room she indicates with her clipboard. She closes the door behind you.

Undress from the waist down. Pull on the cloth hospital gown.

Sit.

Wait.

As you look around, notice a small blue tank, probably oxygen. A face mask. Stainless steel medical instruments on a tray. Glimpse a hint of silver behind a green curtain at the back of the room.

Wonder if that's it—*The Machine.* Do they use a machine? You always thought so. You imagined a vacuum with a long, thin tube and a suction cup at the end. Decide that you don't want to pull the curtain back. You don't want to know how they do it. You just want them to get it over with.

The doctor walks in. Shakes your hand. Tells you his name. Your mind is racing. You don't even hear him explain what's going to happen. Nod when it feels right. Hope he doesn't take too long talking. You've been here almost three hours.

He tells you to lie back on the table. Lie back. Scoot down. A little more. Just a little further. He needs to examine you first.

When the ice-cold metal of the speculum slips in, cry out. Begin bawling, hard. The doctor hesitates.

"We don't have to do this. I can't do this if you don't want me to."

Wave your hand to dismiss him. Explain that the cold hurt. It caught on the walls inside, felt like it scratched you. Feel like an idiot. Wipe your eyes with your sleeve. The arm of a nurse appears from up behind your head, offering you a tissue. Take it. Blow your nose. Feel pathetic having to hand back a dirty Kleenex so they can throw it out for you.

The doctor says he's ready. The same hand reappears holding a mask to your mouth, securing the rubber straps over your ears. The air coming through the mask tastes like plastic. Slowly, the room gets warmer. The sharp edges of the doctor's face and the metal tools begin to blur together.

Feel like you are falling. Try to grasp the edges of the table with your hands. Realize that your hands have gone numb. Do you even *have* hands? Darkness appears around your field of vision. The light shrinks. The room is getting smaller. It's almost the size of a pin; you can see it, a trickle of light at the end of a long tunnel. The doctor's voice comes from farther and farther away.

*Step Ten*

Wake up in one of the reclining armchairs you passed on your way into the operating room. Silently thank whoever decided to give you anesthesia. Look around you. There's a juice box and some crackers on a tray pulled up next to you. The nurse sees you reach for it.

"We find it helps with any nausea or dizziness," she says. She's very nice, warmer than she seemed when she called your name in the waiting room. She says it almost like an apology. As if she is sorry that you're in pain and offering snacks to show her sympathy. Your throat crackles against a thank you.

As you nibble a Saltine, peer at the other girls lying in armchairs. The happy girl from the waiting room is slowly moving her head back and forth, as if trying to shake away a bad dream. She is coming to. Realize that she also had The Procedure. Feel confused, once again, at her nonchalance in the waiting room.

The girl with the tight-lipped mother is still asleep.

They're wheeling in a fourth, older woman. Late thirties, early forties, you guess. Wonder why she needed it, too. Is she a high-powered businesswoman? Can't fit a baby into her career? Did her husband leave her, and she can't do it alone? Is she already struggling with seven kids at home? Was she raped, maybe? You'd understand why she'd had The Procedure, if she'd been raped. You'd be more surprised if she'd kept it.

There are no clues to indicate that any of these stories might be true. She's wearing a hospital gown and no makeup. Her hands are covered with a blanket. You can't if she has a nice manicure or acrylic tips.

As you muse about the woman and what her mystery motive might be, the nurse notices that you are wide awake now. She tells you that you can go in the bathroom and change back into your street clothes. She helps you out of the recliner and guides you to a door opposite the operating room. She offers to help you dress. Tell her you're okay. You can do it.

When she closes the door behind you, collapse onto the toilet seat. Your legs feel like rubber. You really do need help, but were too embarrassed to have anyone else see you naked today. Even partially. Especially from the waist down. Pull your pants over your feet and knees. Use the handicapped bar to gain your balance as you stand up to slide your feet into your shoes. Fold the gown into a neat square and place it in the clothes hamper next to the garbage can.

Open the door. M is waiting for you in the hall. He tells you he pulled the car up to the back entrance. You didn't know the building had a back entrance. The nurse hands you a folder of the same pamphlets that the counselor gave you, along with a list of doctors and numbers you can call in case of emergency. Glance over the list. None are in located your town.

There's a condom taped to the inside pocket of the folder. Smirk at the irony this time. It's the only smile you've cracked in two weeks.

M puts an arm around your shoulder, guides you through a thick metal door into an alley. He left the car running. He opens the door for you. Helps you into the seat. Closes the door behind you. He never does that.

As you exit the alley onto the road, hear a humming sound coming from the parking lot. As you drive past, see a bunch of people carrying signs and shouting at the happy girl as she covers her face and hurries past them.

Protestors.

Whisper, "Thank you, M."

He gives a slight nod. Keeps his eyes on the road.

After a few miles, he asks if you're hungry.

"I guess."

It's almost one. You were in the clinic for almost five hours.

He takes you to Friendly's for lunch.

*Step Eleven*

Sleep for most of the day. Toss and turn for most of the night. Wake up around three a.m. with cramps so bad you feel as if your stomach has burst. Writhe around on the bed. Roll onto your stomach. Onto your back. Onto your stomach. Your side. Curl into a ball. As you do this, recognize the name for this pose. The *fetal* position. Cry through the ache.

Moan. In sorrow. Regret. Blindingly searing pain. Twist around in the sheet so much that you nearly tie a knot in it with your feet.

M brings you some pills and a glass of water. Swallow the Tylenol-3 the doctor prescribed. Take the antibiotics.

Ask M for an extra blanket. Feel comforted as he places the heavy quilt from the living room over you. The weight of it embraces you, hushes you like a warm mother. Know that you go can't back now. You can't take it back. Repeat "Our Father" over and over in your head as if it were a lullaby. It's the only prayer you know.

Softly, cry yourself to sleep.

*Step Twelve*

Find moments of forgiveness.

★★★

Later that year, you are living in a nicer apartment, just as you told M you would. This has been a silent point of contention. When you become pregnant with your daughter that fall, use the calendar to count back to the probable date of conception.

August 4<sup>th</sup>. Caleb's due date.

★★★

Driving home one day, several years later, feel an overwhelming sense of guilt for no reason. Look at the sky on the horizon. Clouds are parting after a summer rainstorm. There's a double rainbow, brighter than anything you've ever seen.

★★★

A few years after that, write your story. Feel as if the words are clawing their way away from your heart and out through your fingertips. The skin on your arms prickles from the inside as you form each sentence, each paragraph. Your stomach wrenches in apprehension. Your eyes keep filling with hot tears that don't fall. Wonder if you're going too far. Wonder if this is really something you want to share.

Realize that you have no choice, as if the story has become its own entity. Refuses to remain in the shadows of the back of your mind any longer. Know that this must be what novelists mean when they say, "The story wrote itself."

Type the words as if they're being dictated to you. The bones in your hands ache from being arched over the keyboard for so long.

As you try to decide whether you should share your story, find one more moment:

Your two-year-old son, with bright eyes and tinkling laughter, clambers onto your lap and hugs you. Kisses you for no reason. Squeaks, "I wuv you, Mommy," before running down the hall to play with his trucks.

## Confession #4

In the animal world,
I would not have eaten you
no matter how bright red sequin,
drooling tinsel curtain, squealing;

we would be wasted
behind layers of acrylic glass, spotlit,
linoleum-toothed tempered smiles.

I would not have eaten you,
having been my own supple flesh,
maroon-spark meat pie
twinkle in my mother's lips;

here, I've seen your teeth
gnashing against the zookeeper.
You devour me, slit-tongued.

## Ma(no)(t)tel

Mother, where are you

when they're calling?

Stage door johnny johns

for you in your hot pants

or your Skipper version:

hot like you, hot like less years,

steamy-young, titty v. breasts young.

Mama, little mama,

stolen halter top

stretched less tight

disco ball glitter eye shadow.

Mother, where are you

when she's sitting at your

on your in your

vanity seat, heavy breathing?

They wanted you first

but isn't it always now

when the mirror betrays:

tube top band aid

coral lipstick tragic clown hair.

Where do you

get deposited, Mother, and how?

and still manage

Skipper's bank slots?

Orange you glad you spray tan?

## Confession #5

People used to compliment me
on your brown ringlet beauty,
ornament, opulent eyes.
When you learned to speak
you would talk to anyone.
I was afraid they'd steal you;
didn't realize you were asking to go.

## *Awake*

I wrapped you once
in poems and songs.

You have kicked away
my blanket of words.

Submerged yourself
in a bathtub of silence.

The water will wrinkle your fingertips
and leave you far less beautiful.

### Conversation on Michigan Ave.

"Yes," she said, "her son died unexpectedly."

As if anyone can prepare for death,
could ever see the sickle moon and think
of a black hood instead
of a broken thumbnail,
or the flame of a candle and wish for
the wisp of silver smoke rather
than the light before it's extinguished.

"A son is hard," answered her friend,
"not like a parent. Dead mothers are a dime a dozen."

We do not expect death, we fear it.
We deny its inevitability.
That is how we can be happy.

Of course, losing a child is harder,
it defies the plan that we are meant to
age before we die, making early death
which itself defies the idea of time
harder to accept, impossible to understand
because it's not as if Death will sit down
in a café explaining his motives in great detail,
outlining his design on a brown napkin

as you sip lattes. Death is too dignified
to risk foam on his upper lip.

"Oh, I agree," said the first. "I think it's easier to recover
from because that's how it's supposed to go."

Go. This is the word that smarts.
Departure, the motion it implies,
as if the swift wind carries
the possibility of arrival,
a destination from which you can send
postcards: *Fun in the Sun—Wish you were here!*
A secluded island where everything is worth
less, except for the children.

## The Prayer Garden

I planted seeds for vegetables, flowers, herbs,
under some delusion that I could become a gardener,
give my life some sort of flavor and nourishment beyond
poetry, speak a new language of dirt and blackened

fingers. Dig and bury, observe the spacing and placement
rules, more sun, no sun, medium sun, partial sun.
The rules of growing are so stringent,
there is no room for life when trying to create it.
I forgot to water them, watered too much,
couldn't distinguish the weeds from the glory.

I am haunted by the cactus I killed. Thinking
it had to rain in the desert every now and then,
I gave it a splash in which it drowned.
I can only now distinguish what I planted
from what is unwanted, because the beauties have browned
and dried; the weeds are flourishing.

Isn't that how it always is? You can only grow what is not
planned.
Plant what you want, and hope it yields just enough
to give you satisfaction, but

even if you can grow something by neglecting it, it still
feels like triumph. You helped by leaving it alone.
So unlike love, so like prayer.

## *Confession #6*

I learned not to speak
when I'm scared or angry,
so I'm loud
when I'm happy
which can be off-putting.

When I'm sad,
       I talk to myself.
You left silence in the wake
of your leaving.
We women
are always left leaving
the girls
       we wish we had been.

I never told you that.

# The Mean Reds

## *Fix*

To repair what is broken;
to sew up the tears;
pick up the pieces,
glue them together,
so only those who look
closely will see
the imperfection.

To settle on or attach securely
to an object or person;
usually a gaze,
a penetrating stare,
eyes focused,
in order to gain
understanding
or peace.

A unit of _____,
usually a substance
to be consumed
in order to quell
a significant desire,
as a drug
or other pleasure.

A difficult situation;
a tight place;
as a moment of stasis
or flux, requiring
a decision to be made.

To secure from change,
vacillation, or wandering;
to place firmly in one spot
as a hand, held tightly,
to show love
or prevent escape.

## Preventing

Before you ask me for more,
and your face clouds
at my dissent and your back
curls over in disgust or fury;

Before you curse me
with your jagged words
and twisted logic rooted
in past negotiations and failures;

Before you present me with
your wounded tongue and
bitter rejection to save face;

Consider that
                    *at least*
I am standing at the epicenter,
at the root of my open stomach.

Consider my clenched fists
ready for action,
ready to pound the empty air,
the pregnant silence.

Consider that I have rage,
even in weakness.

Even in weakness,
consider my rage.

## One Grain

So many times, I
have tried to hold onto
one grain of sand,
all that was left
of my hourglass,
but no matter how
hard I tried,
I was unable
to clean my hands
of the many other grains
that refused to slip
through my fingers.
So, I was left
trying to sort through
the sand I held
trying to decipher
which one grain was
the right one to hold onto.

## *Eating Feelings*

The words for happiness are buoyant,
sharp, crisp like apples
and as sweet:
      exuberant, jubilant, cheerful
so you could bite down
on the sunny yellow, the bright red syllables
and let the juice burst on your tongue.

I prefer the words for sadness,
with their languorousness for the mouth
a slow meal of elegant foods
      melancholy, sorrow, dismal, glum
the grays and blues linger
like fragile china kept in elaborate cupboards,
to preserve their ornamental patterns.

We lock away the delicacy for special occasions,
treat joy like a snack we need to savor.
I find I am consuming far more exotic faire
these days. Empty calories would be welcome.

## Gristle

I have been a participant
in the feasting of my own flesh.
I've painted, tied, and trussed myself
into a juicy roast of succulent flavors.
Stuck my body on the spit.
Invited the teeth to rip
and tear away my glitter skin.
Fricasseed my black lungs,
yellow fingernails, various
holes and treasure troves.
My gray pallor, overcooked
to toughness, but the closest
to silver and sky. Apple
like a ball gag. Splayed
like the butchering's yet to come.

## *With Nothing Left to Consume, I Chose Myself*

At sixteen, I tried to be bulimic:
too much commitment.
One Big Mac curling around itself,
a swirled waste of money,
tangy sauce drip in the corner
of my mouth, reapplied Revlon
Cherries in the Snow lipstick,
pungent red. Still maintained
blue velour belly-shirt flatness.


Learned I couldn't invent
my neuroses, couldn't choose
my disease, depression/anxiety
far less dazzling,
far less Lifetime movie,
more bones-fleshy-white-coconut-mounds,
more pill-rainbow hallucinogen of masks.
I tried to starve myself of insanity:
*anorexiallright*, I'm okay.
Much preferred a blissful week
of wasting chocolate cupcakes,
fingering the creamy center,
fingering my dry paste crushed-ness.

Skinny mirrors villain: whole silver sleek slim

bitches who don't work for it.

Sad mirrors villain: effort, break the broken

first line of offense,

first line out, train out.

I tried to eat myself away,

starve myself sane.

You can devour a chicken,

grease your mind slippery;

can't make the mood thin and smooth

with magenta when you're curving

along the rim of the bowl,

spit out of yourself, your own rejection,

vomiting shards and side effects.

## Paper Doll

So crumpled, over and over
that I cannot be ironed out
or placed between the pages
of a heavy book on a dusty shelf
to erase the crinkles of time and shame
that have etched themselves
into my skin, more each time
in deeper and deeper lines.

I have become soft over the years
from the consistent peppering
of fingertips along my edges,
soft from the folding over
to be made to fit in small pockets.

There are white lines breaking me
into a mosaic picture where I used
to be whole and full of color.

## Piecework

I am getting distracted from the stitching. Should have been sewn back together by now. Self-poppet, doll with pins made for healing. Button eyes staring at nothing. Dress myself. I should have dressed myself this morning, washed myself, sewn myself back together by now. I am still holding pins in my mouth, silencing myself.

Good dolls don't speak, let the play determine the script, let someone else sew, wash, dress, talk for them. I am not a good doll. I haven't finished stitching. I am still half-stuffed, half-dressed, half-sewn, staring at nothing, distracted by the careful practice of repair.

## Melancholy

At some point, we stopped calling it
"melancholia." Clinically: depression,

severe, chronic, seasonal. We gave it
dresses to wear, personalities
to reflect that it was personal
but personable. Like biting a pearl
to see if it's rough (fake) or smooth (real).

Drugged away, talked away, tucked away
into the secret drawer where we also kept
our vibrators and extra boxes of cookies
we'd consume in a single sitting.

We didn't let it be "manic" because
that led to "uncontrollable." *Bipolar.*

Our minds can be like magnets, both
attracting and repulsing themselves.
Always, we are being upended.

Really, the glamour is gone. No glitter
left in the wallow, the only shine's
been dimmed, replaced with small, white.

Even the blueness is medicinal.

## Funereality

Sometimes I don't shower for days,
let my hair get stringy, grease slick
skin, wastewater, sweat vellum,
dirt callous feet, elbow crust,
all my creases gathering ferment.
This is what I'll smell like
when I start to decay.
I'm preparing to be awake
the whole time I'm dying.

## Felling the Orange Tree

I want to be a glamorous disaster:
Faye Dunaway
in a gold ball gown,
destroying the garden—
*Bring me the axe!*—
a small nick on her forehead.

I want to be wearing lipstick,
an inappropriate red,
as I implode:
a million points of light
spreading inward
into nothing.

## Actress

Pretend to be happy.

Wear the mask.

Breathe

> harder,

but act like it's easy.


Dark humor is a good costume.

When it hurts to smile,

> smile.

If you laugh until you cry,

no one will judge you for crying.


*Do not* tell them *anything* real;

when people try to get in,

slam the door shut.

Don't try to help if you weren't asked.

Don't accept help you didn't ask for.


Keep your mouth closed.

Keep your hands closed

> but not into fists.

Let people fuck up—

      if only for the schadenfreude,

      which is your only joy—

so they hurt like you.

Stay away from the good people.

You will eat them alive.


Watch people go by and grit

your teeth at their normalcy.

It's okay to want to punch them in the face.

## On Pathos

There's an effort to feeling, poem after poem, to keep
emoting. Emote, like boat on water, tidal wave, the
struggle to stay afloat. Float the poem. Keep a rubber band
on your wrist and snap it when you're feeling numb (still a
feeling) or feeling too much (which is dangerous for poets).
Feel balance. Try anything to feel like everything. I am
keen to feel, except "feel" sounds like "peel," and I'm too
much in my skin to flay, or slay the keening, which is
another word for feeling too much, and reeling. But stay
up, fly like bird or kite with all your strings struggling to
soar when you're sore from all the feeling. Wind is
everywhere, breezing like breathing. And you have to keep
breathing to keep feeling, and it's the air and the water and
the snapping and the peeling that you keep doing to stay
alive for one more poem that's so exhausting. It's effort, it's
labor to labor a poem into being. Breathe. The pain snaps,
peels glorious layers away. Clarity feels like _____.

## Encase

can't remember, can't feel the fingering against the
spattered skin. frittered, call it breading to close the curtains
and encase yourself. Victorian canopy decadence. There are
times every stretch is felt from a distance, spotlight on
sinew, shuddering. can't feel now in the greasy downturn.
become a burnling, a blister on your own skin. you are,
and are a part of, you. close your mouth, can't feel tongue.
don't want to taste the dark.

## The Flaming Lips Kissed Me Too Hard

Are you the hypnotist
who has come to rid me of my addictions and afflictions?
Will there be a deep chair to fall into?
And a ficus on which to focus as you tell me to relax,
and then a branch to swing from when you tell me I'm a
monkey?
Or a microphone when you tell me I'm Judy Garland?
I always wanted ruby slippers to click my way
home, or someplace different that felt like home.

Will you dangle your pocket watch in my two-handed
face?
Will this blank space, filled with too much time,
ride away on a finger snap
so all I'm left with is calm and ginger snaps?
Will there be a postcard waiting when I return from the
void?
What will my former self have found to say to the now-me
that I may have forgotten, but need to remember?
What will the stamp look like?

Will I recognize you as the magic man who made me
forget?
I will probably steal your pocket watch
to measure the weight of the time you took.

When you pass me on the street,

I may fall backward into that blank space again

if that's the experiment you led me into.

## Wet

I forgot about the bathtub.
Always in the shower,
I forgot about the bathtub:
how coffin, so ready to be red (read),
how full, like a stomach.
Pregnant with hot water (amniotic)
or ready to drown me.

I forgot about the bathtub
and baths with you,
when we washed each other
and slipped fingers lightly
into each other and out.

I forgot about the bathtub
with its white rump curves,
its claw feet scuttling nowhere,
like an animal washed
and quaking with the droplets.

I forgot about the bathtub,
its potential for silence,
threat, comfort.
Always in the shower.
I am avoiding something important.

## *And I Kept My Happy Pills in the Barn*

I lost a farm to my depression.
They took the horse and the plow,
my cows with their too-sweet milk.

The chickens clucked their discontent
as if to say, "You just couldn't
get yourself together. Now

look at your empty yard."
And I saw the coop they'd left—
still, a feather floating in the dusty sunlight.

The machines had taken the last egg,
the fence with the broken slat.
And I turned to the garden—

tomatoes on the cusp of red,
squash vines twisting like my stomach—
and stole someone else's cucumber...

## No Body, No Crime

Scratch that murder.

She never existed,

or she did and was dead already.

An itch so heavy

only a Lizzie Borden waltz would do.

Tool shed and back,

she was just a too-thick log

needing a split down the middle

to feed the kitchen fire.

In the end, it didn't matter

who the killer was

or the intent to make her splinter.

Her blood was invisible.

The gray matter was all flame.

*Dressing*

## One Rule for Line Breaks

Avoid "feminine endings,"
the unaccented syllable.

I am a woman:
I have no accent?
I'm not the last word?

How depressing
that I am not a good line
for even a bad poem.
Or am I a poem at all?

Perhaps I am a syllable.
An unaccented syllable
in a long, lush word
only scholars and poets use correctly

because I am a languorous exercise for the tongue
and the effort I require,
a satisfying medal for the best mouths.

## Under Water

I'm pushing against the surface
  *again.*

Am I drowning?
Is the ceiling made of ice?

I could also be sinking,
headfirst, looking for the bottom.

It stretches me
  and compresses me.
I am pushing to escape
  through my skin
while my skin struggles
to hold me together
  (always like paper
  until I try to rip it).

Am I swimming?
I am not a strong swimmer.
I'm not strong at all.

I just know how to push:
  *past, through, harder, against.*

I can't see the walls
only push
    *up* and *down*
    *out* and *in*
against myself.

I just need to know
which mask to put on
so, I can keep breathing
while I'm down (in?) here.

## Flare

It crawls just under
the skin,
subcutaneous whispers,
electric nerve secrets
needling from the inside,
forcing out from the bones.

It wants to breathe,
break you apart,
explode the capillaries,
make itself a red web
a cartograph of [pain].

It twists around itself,
boils frozen, liquid nitrogen,
if not to escape,
to blast you apart
as if you weren't already shattered.

## Etiquette

Sometimes I invite the pain, a guest
in the home of my nerves. Because I know
I have had it too good, too long. I need to be punished—
flogged with heating pads, strangled with pills—
now, when I know I can take it, serve it
coffee with a plate of fresh cookies.
I have cleaned the house, made it ready

to accept this visitor. It's always better
to be expecting company than to dread the doorbell.
Because then your guest may see the truth,
how you really live:
muddy shoes in the hall, laundry waiting
to be washed and folded,
cobwebs in the ceiling's corners.
You are too polite not to let them in.

Sometimes I invite the pain
because I am lonely
and need someone to talk to.

## Lingering

When we were young and supple,
our bodies low-hanging fruit
ripening in the sun,

it was ours to be angry,
fresh. Our delicate fingers
played preludes to kisses

as we fixed our hair, applied makeup,
that war paint of youth.
We were so obsessed with time,
not knowing what it was

we were waiting for.
We made wishes on everything:
the stars, moon, eyelashes, lucky pennies
for those hands

to move faster, deliver us
from the everlasting present.
Yesterdays were never enough
                    until now.

## *Vice*

Some girls choose food, too much
or too little, until their ribs
become padded cages, or xylophones.
Each bite taken or passed on
is a victory flag that does not fly,
but forces the battle to continue.

There is shopping, stealing, accumulating
nests of names, sewn or painted delicately,
marking a territory conquered where there
has been no country, no civilization for the heart
to build a home within. But there is society
and order in every pocket, stability in stitches.

Others still, choose sex as their modus operandi.
Breasts become their heavy artillery, they arm
their vaginas like snipers waiting for the signal
to take a man down. Glitter is their camouflage,
bed-sheet escape route. If love is a bullet,
they were dead too long ago to remember.

## My Spine

like

telephone cord

neck wrapped

knotted        trip hazard

the other end

of the line

where nerves

screen messages

back,        display

choking red

and blinking:

you are my scoliosis

crooked man

ribs poke discs


no one is calling


the pain is ringing

## When the Angel Leaves the House

She lets the meatloaf burn.
Acrid tire smell poisons the tapestries.
She pulls her pearls from the sink,
like snaking a drainpipe,
dragging up the waste stuck in dark places:
matted hair and bits of fat.

The shirts on the ironing board, waiting
to be rescued—she leaves them wrinkled
and humble. He won't be needing them
to find her. Won't be thinking
how loose the buttons were getting.

She vacuums, just to watch
the dust scattering, dancing
in the sunlight dripping through
the windows she left closed.
Nothing opened but the door—
it was calling, loud as the pills,
but sweeter.

## A Forewarning

I feel the need
to impress upon you
      the fact
that I am real.


Throw away your Pygmalion urges.


I am neither stone statue
nor porcelain doll
for you to craft into
a beautiful image
      of woman,
        of perfection.


I am made of silken flesh
and writhing blood.
My desires burn,
      bonfires
of hopes and promises.


Like seasons I change,
constantly evolving,
becoming and
      unbecoming,
who I feel the compulsion to be.

I cannot be sculpted
or manipulated like clay.
Nor can I be bent
to your whim,
      willow branches
begging to be climbed.

## *Conviction*

We, the perpetually optimistic,
find religion in objects:
a turn of phrase,
the curve of a hip,
a possibility of second chances.
We revel in the black and white catharsis
of screaming with our pens
exorcising our brokenness onto a page.

We huddle in darkened rooms,
cavort in cliques of anonymity.
Escape into worlds where winning
is possible if we distance ourselves
from those who are less broken and
do not see value in hope and promise.
We believe in the good of others' mistakes
and the potential for pessimists
to be proven wrong.

We, who have sat in the company
of the just-as-broken,
been poked at by those who treat us
as if confusion were contagious,
believe in the reincarnation of self,
within one lifetime,

if only to demonstrate that we only need
new beginnings to become great.

We, the perpetually optimistic,
the never-fully-healed,
wear our hearts on our sleeves.
We dress them in perfumes
to protect them from the righteous.
We wear them like name badges,
medals, to display our battle scars
to those who do not understand
our pride in nakedness.

## My Closet is a Castle

I dress as if I've always been pretty
Who was I, before I was?
When did I stop trying to be liked/start saying
*fuckyouyou'remissingout?*

I laugh the way I always have, but now
I can laugh at myself
when I forget my socks
in the shoe store.

I undulate, my tides
have been waiting
for me to rip, and rock.

I pause, dissect myself.
Occasionally
examine the veins in my wrist.
To remind me they are still blue in there.
To remind me they are still there at all.

I have not let my waves crash too far.
Have not forgotten to turn off the engine
when I close the garage door. But
what if I become ugly again?

# ACKNOWLEDGEMENTS

My sincere thanks to editors and staff of the following literary journals which published earlier versions of my work:

*Cellar Door Anthology:* "Preventing"

*Crow Hollow:* "Like a Head" & "With Nothing Left to Consume, I Chose Myself"

*The Manifest Station:* "How to Get Through It"

*Menacing Hedge:* "Funereality," "Gristle," "Felling the Orange Tree," "Dandy," "Igneous Child," "Melancholy"

*Rogue Agent:* "One Rule for Line Breaks"

*Toad Suck Review:* "No Body, No Crime" & "When the Angel Leaves the House"


Additional thanks to LeeAnn Roripaugh, Steve Langan, Audrey Fessler, and Selika Ducksworth-Lawton. Thanks to Kao Kalia Yang for her encouragement to write the scary things. Finally, much love and thanks to my mommy, AMM & SPM.

# MORE TITLES BY JILLIAN PHILLIPS

POETRY

*Pretty the Ugly*

*De-Flowering: Erasure Poetry from Colette's "for a flower album"*

## As Jillie Phillips

SPICY ROMANCE

*One Honest Night* (Spring 2025)

DARK PARANORMAL ROMANCE

*Imaginary Gods* (Summer 2025)

## About the Author

Jillian M. Phillips is a neurodivergent, low-mobility poet and author based in the lush landscapes of Northwest Wisconsin. Her work dives deep into the intersections of sensuality, feminism, and the raw truths of womanhood, drawing comparisons to the evocative style of Sylvia Plath. With a passion for uncovering the beauty in the grotesque and the strength in vulnerability, Jillian's poetry reflects her journey of resilience, exploration, and empowerment.

Jillian's work has been featured in publications such as *Menacing Hedge*, *Crab Fat Magazine*, and *Rogue Agent*, among others. When she's not writing, she can be found blending herbal teas, cultivating creativity, singing karaoke, or reading.

www.ingramcontent.com/pod-product-compliance
Lightning Source LLC
Chambersburg PA
CBHW020418150626
46554CB00014B/1932

* 9 7 9 8 9 9 1 9 5 9 6 1 2 *